ISBN 978-1-5283-2149-5
PIBN 10902628

This book is a reproduction of an important historical work. Forgotten Books uses state-of-the-art technology to digitally reconstruct the work, preserving the original format whilst repairing imperfections present in the aged copy. In rare cases, an imperfection in the original, such as a blemish or missing page, may be replicated in our edition. We do, however, repair the vast majority of imperfections successfully; any imperfections that remain are intentionally left to preserve the state of such historical works.

1 MONTH OF
FREE
READING

at
www.ForgottenBooks.com

By purchasing this book you are eligible for one month membership to ForgottenBooks.com, giving you unlimited access to our entire collection of over 1,000,000 titles via our web site and mobile apps.

To claim your free month visit:
www.forgottenbooks.com/free902628

es / Notes techniques et bibliographiques

L'Institut a microfilmé le meilleur exemplaire qu'il lui a été possible de se procurer. Les détails de cet exemplaire qui sont peut-être uniques du point de vue bibliographique, qui peuvent modifier une image reproduite, ou qui peuvent exiger une modification dans la méthode normale de filmage sont indiqués ci-dessous.

☐ Coloured pages / Pages de couleur

☐ Pages damaged / Pages endommagées

☐ Pages restored and/or laminated /
Pages restaurées et/ou pelliculées

☑ Pages discoloured, stained or foxed /
Pages décolorées, tachetées ou piquées

☐ Pages detached / Pages detachées

☐ Showthrough / Transparence

☑ Quality of print varies /
Qualité inégale de l'impression

☐ Includes supplementary material /
Comprend du matériel supplémentaire

☐ Pages wholly or partially obscured by errata slips, tissues, etc, have been refilmed to ensure the best possible image / Les pages totalement ou partiellement obscurcies par un feuillet d'errata, une pelure, etc., ont été filmées à nouveau de façon à obtenir la meilleure image possible

☐ Opposing pages with varying colouration or discolourations are filmed twice to ensure the best possible image / Les pages s'opposant ayant des colorations variables ou des décolorations sont filmées deux fois afin d'obtenir la meilleure image possible.

L'exemplaire filmé fut reproduit grâce à la générosité de:

Les images suivantes ont été reproduites avec le plus grand soin, compte tenu de la condition et de la netteté de l'exemplaire filmé, et en conformité avec les conditions du contrat de filmage.

Les exemplaires originaux dont la couverture en papier est imprimée sont filmés en commençant par le premier plat et en terminant soit par la dernière page qui comporte une empreinte d'impression ou d'illustration, soit par le second plat, selon le cas. Tous les autres exemplaires originaux sont filmés en commençant par la première page qui comporte une empreinte d'impression ou d'illustration et en terminant par la dernière page qui comporte une telle empreinte.

Un des symboles suivants apparaîtra sur la dernière image de chaque microfiche, selon le cas: le symbole ➔ signifie "A SUIVRE", le symbole ▼ signifie "FIN".

Les cartes, planches, tableaux, etc., peuvent être filmés à des taux de réduction différents. Lorsque le document est trop grand pour être reproduit en un seul cliché, il est filmé à partir de l'angle supérieur gauche, de gauche à droite, et de haut en bas, en prenant le nombre d'images nécessaire. Les diagrammes suivants illustrent la méthode.

3

1

MICROCOPY RESOLUTION TEST CHART

(ANSI and ISO TEST CHART No. 2)

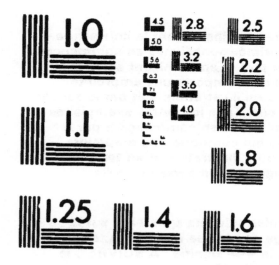

APPLIED IMAGE Inc

1653 East Main Street
Rochester, New York   14609   USA
(716) 482 - 0300 - Phone
(716) 288 - 5989 - Fax

Scientific Demonstration of the Inspiration of the Scriptures 📖

IVAN PANIN'S

SCIENTIFIC DEMONSTRATION
OF THE

INSPIRATION OF THE SCRIPTURES

BY A B. K.
AND FOUR OTHER CLERGYMEN

1915
THE ARMAC PRESS, LIMITED
TORONTO, ONTARIO

PREFACE.

In the folowing pages it is purposed to show that the Christian Bible is constructed on a marvelous numeric design running through its every conceivable detail: that this design could not have originated with man, nor have been carried out by man: that the numeric system on which it is built is similar to the mathematical schemes observed in Nature in the heavens above, or the earth around man. And that this numeric design insures its text against errors and interpolations in much the same way in which the designs on the Bank note are guarded against counterfeits. And as the cash register automatically counts the nickels and the dimes, so this numeric system automatically checks its own accounts.

IVAN PANIN AND HIS BIBLICAL DISCOVERIES.

I.   By A. B. K.

After his conversion, seeking to extend his knowledge of God in Christ, there was revealed to Ivan Panin a fact concealed from the church throughout the ages, but which now demands recognition as the most important by the Church Universal in all its branches, whose creeds are founded on the Bible. Indeed those who have been distressed by many treacherous attacks from so called "scholars" upon the authority of the sacred Scriptures might in view of this wonderful discovery join in singing praises to God. The enemy has come in like a flood that all the foundations might be swept away, but the Lord has placed a standard in the hands of our brother Ivan Panin, and round it all Christian soldiers should rally.

And what is this secret concealed from all other men, including apparently the very writers of the Old and New Testament books?

I once saw a large flourishing tree by the banks of a river. The floods had washed away enough of the bank to expose a wonderful network of entwined roots, the support of the giant tree.

The Bible is a grander Tree of Life, planted "by the streams of (living) water, that bringeth forth fruit in its season."

Digging deep that he might discover precious Scriptural truth, Mr. Panin found to his amazement that the more he dug, the more certain it became that the precious soil he was upturning to the light was extensively filled with the roots of what he has since called *Bible Numerics*. In other words, he found that aside from its revealed facts and teachings the Bible as a literary edifice has a mathematical foundation and superstructure, which underlies and pervades every one of its sixty-six books, and every chapter, often even the single verses in the Hebrew, of each book.

This fact is of such magnitude that only a recital of the numerous illustrative instances Mr. Panin gives from the Hebrew and Greek furnishes the evidence in its volume of facts like rushing, roaring Niagara.

At my request Mr. Panin furnishes here articles easily comprehended by those who cannot read the Bible in its original languages.

You, dear Christian brethren, often harassed and even bewildered by the attack of Higher Critics upon the inspiration of the Bible, may now chase the clouds from your face and let the light of Heaven shine upon it with holy joy and triumph. And you especially, who sorrow at having to sit under sceptical teachers of a mutilated Bible, take heart at the truth here brought to you.

Let me indicate some of the strong points of Mr. Panin's argument, which so far remains unanswered.

There is no stronger argument for the existence of God than the myriads of phenomena which show *design*, and therefore rebuke those who would fain persuade us that the wonders of Creation are produced by blind chance. Now equally wonderful is the exhibition of the mathematical sub-basis of the Bible. This presents an unanswerable argument for the ceaseless presence of the Spirit with Scriptural writers in every word traced by their pens, and in the introduction of Bible numerics on every page and in every paragraph of the Book of Books.

With one notable and three or four minor exceptions, the inspired writers of the Bible were controlled by God's power and wisdom to the introduction of these mathematical forms and figures, *without the least consciousness*, that they were doing what they did. That they once did introduce these numerics would not be significant, but the number of times these sevens, elevens, thirteens, etc., are found intertwined with the very words of the text causes astonishment; and in the spirit of awe and worship we are forced to say this is done by the "finger of God"—not by accident but by the Spirit's design.

Extensive mines of gold, silver, iron, coal,

are known to exist in the bowels of the earth by their *outcroppings*, seen on the surface by the miners. These assure the skilled excavators of the soil that the same Almighty hand which placed these on the surface has placed vast deposits of the same in the now dark interior to be brought to view by the eager pick and shovel of him who digs. Precisely so is it true that there is plainly exposed to view on the *surface* of the Bible an *outcropping* of the numerics which are now found to be characteristic of the interior of the Bible, but concealed until exposed by those who "search the Scriptures." Psalm cxix is exactly such an "outcropping."

This Psalm is almost the only portion of the Bible which as a literary composition is rigidly constructed throughout upon a numeric plan as seen upon the *surface*. The Hebrew alphabet consists of twenty-two letters, which are all made use of by the writer of this Psalm. Under each letter he has exactly eight verses, each of which begins with that particular letter: the entire Psalm thus contains 176 verses, or 22 eights, or 16 elevens. Each of the 176 verses contains a word which is either "law," or its synonym, statute, precept, commandment, etc.

Mr. Panin calls every numeric phenomenon a "feature." Thus in digging *below* the surface of Psalm xc he discovers the first feature to be: "The number of words in this Psalm (without the title) is 63, or 9 sevens." Then Mr. Panin uncovers thirteen more "features" of sevens dug out of Psalm cx. He ends what he has to say upon this Psalm with the words:

"These 14 features of sevens exhaust in no wise the numeric phenomena of this Psalm. But the chance for even these 14 features of sevens being accidental is only one in the 14th power of seven, or one in 678,223,072,849. These numeric phenomena are, therefore,—designed. The time required for constructing a short Psalm *thus* is years. As not a paragraph in the whole Bible, but is constructed similarly, its authorship by ONE MIND, AND A SUPERNATURAL MIND AT THAT, alone accounts for the presence of these phenomena in the Bible."

But Psalm cxix differs from Psalm cx and from nearly all other portions of the Bible in this fact that its author *consciously* and openly brings to the *surface* the numeric features in kind substantially the same as all those others Mr. Panin has brought to light from the *interior* of God's book.

The entire cxix Psalm therefore is an *outcropping* revelation upon the Bible surface of the enormous wealth of Scriptural Numerics which for ages has been concealed from the Church, but is now revealed through our brother Panin. For all of which God is to be praised; for it is indeed a blessing above most blessings needed by the Church Catholic that in this fact of Bible numerics we have not only an unanswerable argument for the plenary inspiration of the whole Bible, but as Mr. Panin shows, the vexed and vexing questions as to Bible chronology, questions as to Christ's genealogy in Matthew and Luke, questions as to Vocabularies, spellings, questions as to titles of Psalms, and many other questions, are finally settled by Bible Numerics.

One thing is now beyond all doubt: namely, that, in the language of Mr. Panin, "Inspiration alone. Inspiration by a superhuman mathematical mind. the Mathematical Author of Creation, alone accounts for the presence of these phenomena in the Bible."

May we not hope that after reading the following pages by Mr. Panin, collegians and theological students will be induced to study his more voluminous and scholarly works written for those acquainted with the Hebrew and Greek languages?

It is thought best that the following highly pertinent comments on the work of Mr. Panin precede his own presentation of the case. The four clergymen represent four different Evangelical bodies: Congregational, Presbyterian, Methodist Protestant, and the Christian Connection. Dr. Turney is the official Polemic of the Methodist Protestant Church of America; Dr. Summerbell, for years the editor of their official organ, is recognized by all as by far the ablest writer and most accomplished scholar in the Christian Connection.

Mr. Swinnerton, moreover, does not speak as one who has merely heard Mr. Panin and read his work. Himself a Hebrew and Greek scholar, he has, before committing himself, specially in print, thoroughly tested Bible Numerics for himself; and has since done valuable original work in the rich field thus opened by Mr. Panin. He therefore surely speaks with peculiar authority. While Mr. Moore's case is the more striking in that he came to hear Mr. Panin highly prejudiced against the novel teaching. While Dr. Turney has gone even further than Mr. Swinnerton. He has not only verified Ivan Panius' work, but he has examined the Iliad for numerics without result, and has spent days in constructing a letter of his own with Scripture numerics, only to meet with the same failure.

Three out of these four clergymen thus give here not only their mere opinions about Bible Numerics, but their actual experience therewith. They have all found, to use Mr. Swinnerton's joyful exclamation after his own first test of Numerics, that *It works!*

II. W. T. SWINNERTON, IN *Stamford (Conn.) Daily Advocate.*

Mr. Panin to my mind proves that the student of the Scriptures has now something more than the mere subjective persuasion that they are inerrant and textually as well as spiritually infallible, a persuasion he cannot impart to another, and by which he can neither convince nor silence the obdurant objector. He produces a convincing array of facts objective to himself to which he can appeal, and which no living man has yet attempted to dispute, and which cannot fail to carry the assent of any normal intellect or of one capable of using his mathematical faculties. When it is said that the evidence adduced to establish this stupendous fact of verbal inspiration can be verified by any one even slightly acquainted with the original text of Scripture, and can also be made plain to any other man of ordinary intelligence; and again that the evidence is actually coercive of intellectual assent beyond the suspicion of a peradventure: then men of all shades of belief and of non-belief and unbelief are expected to sit up and take notice.

Overwhelming as are his facts even in dry, cold print, in his addresses on the topic of Scripture Numerics they become thrilling. He there presents quietly and plainly, yet most attractively, with or without the aid of a blackboard, the result of many years of absorbing study and concentrated research of the Scriptures in the languages in which they were originally given to men. He there first points out that science and certain experiences and observations common to all men show that the Universe, so far as it has disclosed itself to human inquiry, is built upon mathematical principles: that the Author of Nature is a most marvellous mathematician. If the Creator, whose glory the heavens declare, chose to produce a book, —whether He has or not is a subject of legitimate inquiry—would it not be produced on the same principles of mathematical perfection, so that he can say: "The law of the Lord is perfect?'' As no man can claim to be the creator of the mathematical wonders of the heavens, so God has written His signature in His Word that no man can claim it as a human production. The Bible which you carry in the pocket, which you open before the Sunday School class, which is upon the pulpit and from which the minister takes his text every Sunday, which you read to the sick or quote at the bedside of the dying, this book which you open to lead an inquiring soul into light and to the eternal Light Himself,—is shown by the most scrutinizing demonstration to be the result of the divine fiat, extending to letters, words, paragraphs, and books, and to the whole Bible as a unit.

Forevermore it remains true that the entrance of God's Word gives light; and the man of God is thereby thoroughly furnished unto every good work. The establishment of the inerrancy and infallibility of the Scriptures, which the Fathers lived upon, and in the hope of which they died, and which their sons are trying both to live and die without, is freighted with the most momentous and appalling consequences to a vast body of literature enshrined in Bible dictionaries, encyclopedias, and commentaries; and to whole libraries of the output of the modern religious press. ''The grass withereth, the flower fadeth; surely the people is grass, but the Word of our God shall stand forever.''

Old, old words receiving comforting corroboration in these latter days! The common people need no longer wait upon dictatorial scholarship for its last guess; and, as they wait, shiver in the chill of a half faith. The extraordinary numerical structure of the Scriptures is now demonstrated.

With the first eleven verses of the first chapter of Matthew, for example, Mr. Panin illustrates in his lectures the plan that pervades the entire Scripture, with comparative references to other parts of Scripture. He shows that the Greek text is constructed on an elaborate system of multiples of seven. The same mathematical phenomena extend to all parts of the text, vocabulary, grammatical forms of words, their distribution in gender, in parts of speech, in comparative frequency of occurrences. It is seen also in special sub-divisions of a paragraph, such as a speech in the midst of the narrative; and, what is still more surprising, in the arithmetical value of the various words found in the entire chapter. Each of these particulars exhibits the same extraordinary mathematical design. And the same marvellous phenomena are found to prevail not only in dislocated portions of Scripture, but throughout the entire book.

Mr. Panin shows the utter impossibility of such a mathematical design being the work of mere man. An incidental result of the application of this universal law of mathematical design is the possibility of producing at last the autograph text as it came to the prophets and apostles from the inspiration of God. Such a result is surely stupendous. Critics have been telling us a great deal about the original auto graphs. They tell us that they are lost, undiscoverable; that no crypt has surrendered this priceless treasure; and should it be brought to light, it would be met by the onslaught of the whole school of destructive criticism. In our youthful days, how the enemy flayed us with his unanswerable taunt that our best and oldest manuscripts were both corrupt and modern? The stamp of modernity upon the precious documents from which our English Bible came lay like a blight upon our only heirloom and heritage. Now, however, a perfect text can be obtained. The key of Bible Numerics detects at once the true; and at the same time reveals how wonderfully perfect are the priceless words which are the god-given boon of the church.

The section of Scripture strangely lost from manuscripts (John 7:53 - 8:11) is shown by the science of Numerics to belong to the Scriptures. Every one felt that it was entitled to its place even if the Revisers signified their doubt, and enclosed it in brackets. Now, however, we know that this priceless gem belongs in reality to the original text of Scripture, and is not to be erased or even disfigured by brackets. Numerous other examples, like the Last twelve Verses of Mark, the agony in the garden, the first prayer from the Cross, all now conclusively shown by Mr. Panin to be true Scripture, may be adduced to show that at last we may yet come to have an indestructible and inerrant text.

III. DR. J. J. SUMMERBELL.

IN THE *Herald of Gospel Liberty.*

The very hairs of your head are all numbered. So said Jesus. He was not trifling. Your very hairs are counted (*arithmeo.*) It is the very word from which our English word *arithmetic* comes.

If God counts the hairs on our heads, he *may* count the words of his Scripture amanuenses, and guide them to interesting combinations of numbers.

He counts the five fingers on our hands, the five toes on our feet, the five senses we daily use; he counts the seven days of the week, the seven churches in Asia, the seven so-called "lost books," the "seven golden candlesticks," the "seven spirits of God," the seven seals of Revelation, the seven lamps and the seven plagues; he counts the twelve tribes of Israel, the twelve foundations of Jerusalem and its gates, the twelve apostles, and the twelve baskets of fragments after feeding thousands; he counts the forty years Moses was in Egypt, the forty years he was in Midian, the forty years he led Israel, the forty days he was in the mount with God; he counts the forty days it rained with Noah, the forty days respite before Nineveh could be destroyed, the forty days' fasting of Elijah, the forty days' temptation of Jesus, and his tarrying forty days after his passion; well! yes; God is all the time counting.

The leaves of the tree encircle the stem with

a certain number; the elements in chemical action unite or divide by count; the radius vector of the planet describes equal areas in equal times. Look where you will, if we find God at work, we find Him counting. He is the Great Arithmetician. He is counting, ever counting; the days the egg must be warmed to life, the days the fever must heat toward death, and the very pulse beats of the patient, as he sinks into the condition where there is no counting. The divine beings are always counting: the mason as he lays the brick in the wall, Jesus as they gather up the fragments that remain, and the Mighty One who "hath *measured* the waters in the hollow of his hand, and *meted* out the heaven with a *span*, and comprehended the dust of the earth in a *measure*, and *weighed* the mountains in *scales*, and the hills in a *balance*."

Seeing that God counts the petals in the springtime, the sides of the honey-bee's cell in the summer, the lines of frost on the window pane in the autumn, and the angles of the snowflake in the winter, we were not quick to reject the theory of our honored Russian brother, Ivan Panin, as shown in the HERALD OF GOSPEL LIBERTY by our beloved English brother, W. J. Warrener; but we opened our eyes, looked intently, were interested, even as in the counting in nature's pages: though we were not prepared either to advocate or reject the theory. If true, it is important. The investigation cannot be unworthy, which brings out mathematical treasures from God's word, if it be admitted that Darwin is to be commended for finding something interesting in an earth-worm. The great question is, Is the contention of Ivan Panin true? . . . .

No one can look at a brick wall and not see design in it. If there is a certain number of bricks in every course, we think it is intended. If, now, we should come across a certain wall that looked like a history, that told a plain story, picturing events so plainly that a child could understand them; and if the bricks came from different brickyards, were of different sizes, and of different shapes, and yet we could all read the story—surely we would be more deeply interested if we should find that the number of bricks were always the same in a course. Now in addition to all that, suppose that we should find that the wall had the property of giving life to all diseased persons who would look at it, we would admire the wall still more. Suppose, also, some humble admirer of the mason should carefully survey the wall, count the number of courses, the number of headers, of joints, of corners, of filling bricks, and then inform us that the bricks were all arranged arithmetically:—would we not be deeply impressed! Suppose there had been long controversy about this wall and efforts made to belittle it; but it held together, and produced such a moral influence on the community by its picture and story, that men considered it built by a Divine Mason. Would the discovery of the mathematical arrangement of the bricks all through the wall detract any from its impressiveness? Would it not add to the usefulness of the wall to have it found out that by a careful observance of the construction of the wall it could be determined whether the improvements of the higher critics were true, and which bricks in supposed rubbish on the ground really belonged to the wall? . . . . .

Panin is eminently open and scientific. He proceeds according to the true scientific method, in the modern approved ways. He bases all on observed facts: on scores, on hundreds, on thousands. Of these facts he asks the most careful examination. We have conversed with him, we have seen some of his data. He is scientific. Like the true work of a scientific man it leads to other truth. For instance: In counting the word *Moses* in the Concordance, he found it 79 times, and it did not harmonize with the principle. He had already become convinced of the system of numerics as divine, and at once doubted the concordance, the most accurate up to that time. He read the New Testament through, to find if that was the number of times the word *Moses* occurred. He found it 80 times; the concordance having been wrong. The number 80 dovetailed to all the rest.

If Panin's theory is true, personally we will be compelled to change some views we have long held, but we will be glad to have the added light.

Jesus said, " Till heaven and earth pass away

one jot or one tittle shall in nowise pass away from the law till all things be accomplished." He was speaking of the Old Testament. If its least letter was so important, we may not be afraid to count the New Testament. "Open thou mine eyes, that I may behold wondrous things out of thy law."

Later:—Since the foregoing was in type, we have had the privilege of hearing a lecture on this subject by Ivan Panin himself. It was really thrilling to all the audience. The modern scientific spirit could not but be recognized, and a scientific master. Higher critics may not like the idea, but there is true science.

2.

Some persons do not understand Panin's theory, partly because he is so familiar with the subject that his articles nearly always begin with no statement of his theory; but with a statement of some dry statistics that have no interest revealed until the closing sentences of the article. Their meaning does not appear till then. Panin's interest is in the *facts* he presents; which are to him the matter now to be gathered. It is evident that he is not deeply concerned to make plain his theory. He seems intent to flood the learned men and objectors with *facts*. This is the true scientific spirit. It is not a *priori*.

The only scholarly objection that we have yet noticed has been based on reading numerics into certain poems. Panin would not object at all to this: for the poets considered have numerics by *design*. And that is Panin's point: the numerics show design. And the numerics in the Scriptures are not obvious, like the numerics of the feet of a poet. The Bible numerics are only discovered by scientific and scholarly Investigation; like the number of the plant's leaves on the twig, when fully compassing the circumference; like the arithmetic of the musical scale of the human voice; like the arithmetic of the solar system; like the arithmetical arrangement of chemical atoms in a molecule. All know that the discovery of this wonderful distribution of arithmetic in the phenomena of nature has been a great factor in the overthrow of atheism, which has been so complete that atheists are now rare; agnosticism being the present day refuge of the defeated opposers of a God.

We once requested a college professor of Greek to take up some Greek prose classic and ascertain if he could make Panin's theory work on it. But we have not heard from him on the subject. . . . .

Scholars must hereafter reckon with Panin.

IV. E. H. MOORE, *before the Minister's Meeting of St. Paul, Minn.*

When a brilliant and scholarly man who renounces a successful career because of principle and for conviction's sake gives his life to the study and impartation of Truth, even Truth newly discovered; Truth, as he believes, that

will objectively prove the plenary inspiration of
the word of God, which we all profess to love
and accept as the only infallible rule of faith
and practice; when such a man, who is surely
a numerical genius, believes he has discovered
an elaborate and marvellous plan in the letters,
words, books, and complete whole of Scripture,
which will determine absolutely the true text,
words and passages, and even the arrangement
of the books,—we to whom at the outset this
may seem novel and phantastic, ought not to
draw back in our superior ignorance and refuse
even a hearing to one who may indeed have discovered the truth of God; and whose rejection,
if he be and have what he claims, may prove
our intellectual and spiritual loss here, and
something for which we must give account to
the great God, the interpretation of whose revealed truth we have superciliously spurned.

When I first heard of Mr. Panin and his
numerical scheme I was as much prejudiced as
any man might be. I thought of Origen and
his allegorical interpretations of Scripture, and
of Mr. Totten and his mathematics concerning the end of the world. Since hearing and
knowing Mr. Panin my feeling has changed. . . .

In addition to the scheme of sevens which he
points out in every paragraph of Scripture very
elaborately in his publications, there are many
others, wheels within wheels, combinations sim-
ple and complex, kaleidoscopic in character.
The author is everywhere clear, logical, and

convincing. There is nothing of the crank or special pleader.

I confess that the thought of the possibility of this scheme being true has made the Word of God seem more real and sacred to me. In a deeper sense does the passage appeal to me: The Scripture cannot be broken: and again: Not one jot or tittle shall pass away till all be accomplished. He who fills all nature with numbers and rhythmic schemes (so much so that Pythagoras thought numbers the elements of all things, and not of music only), certainly would be likely to make His *written* revelation to betray the same genius of numbers.

V. DR. DANIEL B. TURNEY
IN THE *Herald of Gospel Liberty.*

A world of valuable truth has been unearthed by Ivan Panin concerning the numerics of the Bible.

The arithmography of Scripture is the death warrant of the theory of the destructive critics. The numerics worked out by Ivan Panin are fatal to the foes of verbal inspiration, and are invulnerable.

My own examinations of the arithmography of Scripture sustain so emphatically the claims and conclusions of Ivan Panin, that I take pleasure in openly commending his work, as presenting facts and evidences which no destructive critic can successfully face.

A sincere effort to find numerics in Homer's

Iliad proved unsuccessful; but as soon as I tried 3 John, my labors were rewarded abundantly. I took up this book because it is short; and in Panin's writings I had not seen it discussed. My investigation began therefore with as little to guide me as in the case of the Iliad, but the result was so perfect a scheme of numerics that I have not a shadow of doubt as to the truth of Ivan Panin's theory.

I cannot close my eyes to the clear evidence of design plainly beyond the purpose, or even the knowledge of the penman; and woven into the sacred oracles for use in a century in which destructive critics would treat the whole Book with the same rashness that characterizes Dr. Gledden's treatment of the book of Esther.

I tested this matter for myself thus: I gave numerical values to the English alphabet, and tried to prepare a letter which would adhere to the numerics, and make every section a multiple of seven, and present all the other features of the arithmographic septology of the Bible, without descending to nonsense. My letter scale ran: a, 1; b, 2; c, 3; d, 4; e, 5; f, 6; g, 7; h, 8; i, 9; j, 10; k, 20; l, 30; m, 40; n, 50; o, 60; p, 70; q, 80; r, 90; s, 100; t, 200; u, 300; v, 400; w, 500; x, 600; y, 700; z, 800, a close approach to the Hebrew and Greek scales. But after working for days on it, I could get no satisfaction. Yet this feat is accomplished in every one of the thousands of bible paragraphs without the slightest visible effort. How was this done? By *design*. But neither the Greek

nor the Hebrew writers were capable of forming such a design. They were incapable in
themselves of carrying out such a design, if
other men had formed it for them. But *God*
could form such a design and carry it out using
the human penmen as instruments.

I see clearly in these numeric phenomena the
exposure and overthrow of the false assumption
that underlies the whole hypothesis of the destructive critic. When anything of pre-eminent
worth appears, it seldom so comes as to at first
strikingly to engage general attention. The
wondrous well is not always found by the sages,
as the four-leaved clover at the doorstep may be
overlooked by the very one in quest thereof.

The rationalists of Germany undertook to
account for the moral truths in the Bible without Inspiration, just as the agnostic evolutionist
undertook to explain the order and harmony of
Nature without a Designing Mind. They have
reckoned without their host. God raised up
Ivan Panin, and through him pointed to an
arithmography pervading the Bible, which pro-
tects it against interpolation and alteration. The
inspiration of the Bible, its being the production
of one Designing Mind, is now clearly and con-
vincingly established.

Bible Numerics is the key to the situation,
and it furnishes the final criterion for nearly all
questions raised about the Bible.

SOME NUMERIC PHENOMENA OF THE BIBLE.

BY IVAN PANIN.

I.

1. I have been asked to furnish some examples of those numeric phenomena in the structure of the Bible the presence of which cannot be accounted for by ascribing them to ɪere man. In the original languages in which the Bible is written—the Hebrew for the Old Testament, the Greek for the New—every page, every paragraph, and in the Old Testament often even only a single verse, may be said without exaggeration to be teeɪing with those numeric phenomena which are duplicated only in that other Book of God, the visible Creation. And I have been asked, moreover, to give only such examples as can be understood by readers of the English, and if need be verified also by one who cannot read the Bible in its original languages.

2. Let us then turn to the English Bible, and look at the phenomena to be observed on even its very surface. It consists of the following books:

(As the argument is not affected by the change the *order* of the books is for convenience given as they stand in the Hebrew and Greek..

The Old Testament books are these:

1	Genesis	21	Nahum
2	Exodus	22	Habakkuk
3	Leviticus	23	Zephaniah
4	Numbers	24	Haggai
5	Deuteronomy	25	Zechariah
6	Joshua	26	Malachi
7	Judges	27	Psalms
8	1 Samuel	28	Proverbs
9	2 Samuel	29	Job
10	1 Kings	30	Canticles
11	2 Kings	31	Ruth
12	Isaiah	32	Lamentations
13	Jeremiah	33	Ecclesiastes
14	Ezekiel	34	Esther
15	Hosea	35	Daniel
16	Joel	36	Ezra
17	Amos	37	Nehemiah
18	Obadiah	38	1 Chronicles
19	Jonah	39	2 Chronicles
20	Micah		

The New Testament books are:

40	Matthew	54	2 Corinthians
41	Mark	55	Galatians
42	Luke	56	Ephesians
43	John	57	Philippians
44	Acts	58	Colossians
45	James	59	1 Thessalonians
46	1 Peter	60	2 Thessalonians
47	2 Peter	61	Hebrews
48	1 John	62	1 Timothy
49	2 John	63	2 Timothy
50	3 John	64	Titus
51	Jude	65	Philemon
52	Romans	66	Revelation
53	1 Corinthians	2,211.	

3. Not all these books give the names of their writers. In fact a whole third of these books are anonymous. There is, for example, every reason for believing that Genesis has Moses for its author, but Genesis itself does not say so; neither is it anywhere in the Bible clearly asserted that *he* wrote it. Likewise Lamentations is generally believed to be a work of Jeremiah, but from the Bible itself we do not yet know it. The prophecy of Jeremiah assigns itself distinctly to Jeremiah, but not Lamentations. If the writer of this book is to be discovered it must be in some other way than by direct statement of the Bible itself. In the same way there is every reason for believing that Matthew wrote the book of Matthew, that Mark wrote Mark, that Luke wrote Luke and Acts, that Paul wrote Hebrews. But all this cannot yet be shown from the Bible itself. In other words, as far as the testimony of the Bible itself goes, these books and some others are anonymous.

4. But in the following books their writers are named as such either in the books themselves wholly or in part, or elsewhere in the Bible. Thus Psalms was not indeed wholly written by David, but a large portion thereof was; and the book as a whole is spoken of in the New Testament as David's. The same is true of Exodus, Leviticus, Numbers, and Deuteronomy, in their relation to Moses. Portions of these do ascribe themselves to Moses, and at

least these four books are quoted in the Bible as the work of Moses. The following, accordingly, are the books of the Bible which are thus distinctly assigned therein to their respective authors: Exodus, Leviticus, Numbers, Deuteronomy—to Moses; Isaiah, Jeremiah, Ezekiel, the twelve so called minor prophets, Daniel, Ezra, Nehemiah, James, 1 Peter, 2 Peter, Jude, ascribe themselves to the writers whose names they respectively bear. Thirteen of the Pauline Epistles ascribe themselves to Paul. Psalms is ascribed to David. Proverbs and Canticles ascribe themselves to Solomon; Ecclesiastes ascribes itself to "the son of David"; Revelation, to John. The anonymous books thus are: Genesis, Joshua, Judges, 1 and 2 Samuel, 1 and 2 Kings, Job, Ruth, Lamentations, Esther, 1 and 2 Chronicles, Matthew, Mark, Luke, John, Acts, 1, 2 and 3 John, Hebrews.

5. Of the Old Testament writers the following are expressly named as such in the New: Moses, Isaiah, Jeremiah, Hosea, Joel, David, Daniel. The names of two other Old Testament writers are indeed found in the New, Solomon and Jonah; but these are not named as *writers*, and no quotations from their books accompany the mention of their names. They are named only as Old Testament characters among others. But these seven are expressly cited as Bible writers in the New Testament.

6. Of the persons named as its writers in

the Bible some have more than one book ascribed
to them. Thus Moses has 4, Solomon 3, Peter
2, Paul 13. The other writers have only one
book ascribed to each: namely, the 16 prophets
so called, David, Ezra, Nehemiah, James, Jude,
and John.

7. In the list of Bible Books given above
in Sec. 2 the 66 books have the numbers 1-66 set
against them, so that each book has thus that
number set against it which designates its place
in the order of the books as they are found in
the Bible. This number is for convenience
hereafter spoken of as the *order number* of that
particular book. Thus the order number of
Genesis is 1, it being the first book of the Bible;
that of Revelation is 66, it being the last; the
order number of Matthew is 40, it being the
fortieth book, and so for the rest.

8. In Sec. 2 it was already pointed out that
in the *order* of the books the English Bible
departs from the original. And it differs there-
from in one other respect: In the original languages the Bible consists of marked divisions;
those of the Old Testament being even stamped
with the authority of the Lord Jesus himself.
In the Hebrew Bible, namely, the Old Testament books are divided into three great divisions: the Law, Prophets, [Holy] Writings.
Genesis-Deuteronomy, the Law; Joshua-Mal-
achi, the Prophets; Psalms-Chronicles, the
Writings. "All things written of me in the

Law of Moses, and the Prophets, and the Psalms," in Luke 24:44 refers to this division: the third division being designated by the book at its head. The New Testament in its turn falls into four great divisions: Gospels, Acts, Epistles, Revelation.

9. Of the 66 books of the Bible 21 are Epistles themselves: the seven so called Catholic, the fourteen Pauline. But the following twelve books, while not letters themselves, contain letters: 2 Samuel, 1 and 2 Kings, Isaiah, Jeremiah, Esther, Daniel, Ezra, Nehemiah, 2 Chronicles, Acts, Revelation. For convenience these twelve books will hereafter be spoken of as the Epistolary books, as distinguished from the Epistles themselves.

With these preliminaries thus out of the way we can now proceed to the numeric phenomena themselves.

10. Now the first fact in Bible numerics to be noticed here is that the number of books in the Bible is 66, or 6 *elevens* (Feature 1): of these the anonymous books are 22 in number, or 2 *elevens*: and the non-anonymous books are 44 in number, or 4 *elevens* (Feature 2). And of these 44 non-anonymous books 22, or 2 elevens, belong to writers of more than one book, and 22 to writers of only one book (Feature 3). The books without Epistles are 33 in number, or 3 elevens: the Epistles and Epistolary books are also 33 (Feature 4).

That is to say: the whole number of Bible

books being a multiple of eleven, it is divided between books naming their authors and books not naming them, between books belonging to only one author and books belonging to more than one, between books with letters and books without, by—elevens.

11. The sum of the 66 order numbers of the 66 Bible books (see Secs. 2 and 6) is 2,211, or 201 elevens, which is divided thus by elevens: the 22 books of the authors of more than one book have 946, or 86 elevens; the other 44 books have 1,265, or 115 elevens (feature 5).

That is to say: Just as the number itself of the books is divided by elevens between books belonging to writers of only one book and those belonging to writers of more than one, so their *order* numbers are also distributed between the two classes by elevens.

12. Of the books that are wholly Epistles the order numbers are 45-65. Now this sum 2,211 for the 66 books is thus divided between Epistles and non-Epistles: non-Epistles have 1,056, or 96 elevens; Epistles, 1,155, or 105 elevens (feature 6). And of the Epistles the *first, middle* and *last* books have 165, or 15 elevens (feature 7) of which in turn the first and last have 110, or 10 elevens; and the middle has 55, or 5 elevens (feature 8).

That is to say: Just as the number itself of the Bible books is divided between books consisting of or containing letters and the other books by elevens, so their order numbers also are divided by elevens between Epistles and non-Epistles.

13. Of the sum of the order numbers of the Epistles just seen to be 1,155, or 105 elevens, numbers 53, 54, 55, 59, 60, are addressed to churches directly namely: 1 and 2 Corinthians, Galatians, 1 and 2 Thessalonians; 65 is addressed to Philemon, and also to *the church in thy house*. In 50, namely 3 John, the writer states that he had written somewhat *to the church*, but "Diotrephes who loveth to have the pre-eminence among them receiveth us not." The sum of the order numbers of these seven church or semi-church Epistles is 396, or 36 elevens (Feature 9). And if we arrange these numbers in their proper order, 50, 53, 54, 55, 59, 60, 65, the middle one is found to be 55, or 5 elevens (Feature 10).

14. It was shown above in Sec. 8 that the Bible consists of seven great divisions. These seven divisions begin with these books: Genesis, Joshua, Psalms, Matthew, Acts, James, and Revelation. They end with Deuteronomy, Malachi, 2 Chronicles, John, Acts, Philemon, and Revelation. The order numbers of these books, 1, 5, 6, 26, 27, 39, 40, 43, 44, 45, 65, 66, have for their sum 407, or 37 elevens (Feature 11). These seven divisions of the Bible consist, moreover, of two classes: those consisting of more than one book, and those consisting of only one book each, namely Acts and Revelation. Now this sum 407, or 37 elevens, is thus divided: the divisions consisting of more than one book

have 297, or 27 elevens; the divisions which consist of only one book each, Acts and Revelation, have 110, or 10 elevens (feature 12). And of this number again Acts has 44, or 4 elevens; and Revelation has 66, or 6 elevens (feature 13).

Hitherto only the books themselves and their order numbers have been considered. Let us now look at the names of the Bible writers.

15. The persons named in the New Testament as writers of the Old (See. 5 above) are the authors of books with the following order numbers: 2, 3, 4, 5, 12, 13, 15, 16, 27, 35. Their sum is 132, or 12 elevens (feature 14). While the two writers whose names occur in the New Testament, but not as of Old Testament *writers*, Jonah and Solomon, have for the sum of the order numbers of their books 110, or 10 elevens (feature 15).

16. In addition to the seven Old Testament writers spoken of in the New (See. 5), the following persons are named therein as *New Testament* writers: James, Paul, Peter, Jude, and John. Now the names of these twelve Bible writers named in the New Testament are found in the whole Bible 2,871 times, or 261 elevens (feature 16), of which the Old Testament writers have 2,310, or 210 elevens; and those of the New Testament 561, or 51 elevens (Feature 17). And Mosses, who is the first Bible writer, has 847, or 11 x 11 x 7, a multiple of eleven (feature 18) elevens (feature 19).

17. The seven names of these Old Testament writers occur thus: Moses is found in 31 books; Isaiah in 12; Jeremiah in 8; Hosea in 7; Joel in 7; Daniel in 6; David in 28. The sum of these numbers in 99, or 9 elevens (Feature 20), of which the *first*, *middle* and *last* (compare feature 7 above) have 66, or 6 elevens (feature 21).

The name of the <u>first</u> of these seven writers, Moses, occurs in the Bible, as has been stated, 847 times. In some books it occurs more than a hundred times, thus requiring a number of three figures to express it. In Exodus, for example, it occurs 290 times. In others, however, it occurs less than a hundred times, but a number requiring two figures to express it; as in Joshua, where it occurs 58 times. In others again it occurs less than 10 times, thus requiring only one figure to express it. Now the 21 books where Moses is found a number of times small enough to be expressed by one figure have this name 77 times, or 7 x 11; and the books with the numbers of more than one figure have 770, or 11 x 7 x 10. The division here is not only by elevens, but by seven elevens (feature 22).

Again: as already seen in Sec. 12 and elsewhere, the Epistles form a marked division of the Bible. Now the 847 occurrences of Moses in the Bible are thus divided by elevens: the non-Epistles have 825, or 75 elevens; the Epistles have 22, or 2 elevens (feature 23). And of this number Hebrews, where it occurs most, has eleven (feature 24).

In connection then with the mere number of
Bible books, their order numbers, and the occurrences in the Bible of the names of some of its
writers no less than 24 distinct features of
elevens are to be observed.

18.   These 24 features of elevens are here:
they are a fact.   They may prove interesting
or uninteresting, desirable or undesirable; but
our first business with them is to accept them
as a—fact.

Now this fact, the presence here of these 24
features of elevens is either accident or design.
As only every eleventh number is a multiple of
eleven, the chance for any particular number
being a multiple of eleven is only one in eleven,
since the matter being left to chance, the other
ten numbers have as good a chance to merely
happen as this particular multiple of eleven.
So that the chance for any one of the 24 features
of elevens to merely happen here is only one
in eleven; the chance for any two features of
elevens to just happen here is only one in 11 x 21,
or one in 231; the chance for any three features
of elevens to just happen here is only one in
11 x 16 x 31, or one in 5456.   The chance for
every additional feature of eleven thus dimishes
some twenty-five fold.   Going thus through all
the 24 features of elevens enumerated thus far,
their occurrence here accidentally *rather than
by design*, is just one in 263 x 257 x 251 x 248
x 244 x 241 x 131 x 127 x 123 x 83 x 65 x 43
x 37 x 35 x 29 x 27, a number requiring some
thirty figures to express

When the odds against anything merely happening run into even only a million, it is already deemed highly improbable that it just happened, when they run into a hundred millions, it is held as practically certain, that no mere chance was here at work; when the chances against a thing being accidental rather than designed are some *billion millions taken a million million times*, rational men do not even think of ascribing it to chance.

If a dozen buttons were to be found on the street all in a row, no one would think that as they fell out they just arranged themselves *by chance* into that row. And were that dozen buttons found not in one row of twelve, but in two rows of six, or three rows of four, no reasonable person would risk his reputation for sanity by denying that these rows were *made* there by some one. And here are not two-three such rows, but twenty-four of them.

The presence here of these 24 features of elevens, therefore, is not accident but design.

An elaborate scheme of elevens is thus seen to run through the mere number of the Bible books, their order numbers, and the names of some of its writers.

19. But side by side with this elaborate scheme of elevens an equally elaborate scheme of *sevens* is displayed here:

It has already been seen above (Sec. 8) that the Bible falls into seven great divisions (Feature 1): Law, Prophets, Hagiagrapha, Gospels,

Acts, Epistles, Revelation. The Law having 5 books, Prophets 21, Hagiagrapha 13, Gospels 4, Acts 1, Epistles 21, Revelation 1. The largest divisions contain each 21 books, or 2 sevens (Feature 2). The Epistles, one of these two largest divisions, are divided thus: Seven are addressed to, or connected with, churches as such (Feature 3, see Sec. 9 above). The so-called Catholic are seven in number, the Pauline Epistles are 14, or 2 sevens (Feature 4). These Pauline Epistles are addressed to bodies, or individuals. Now they are addressed to just seven specified bodies: to Romans, Corinthians, Galatians, Ephesians, Philippians, Colossians, Thessalonians (Feature 5). Their order numbers are 52-60, their sum 504, or 72 sevens (Feature 6).

20. In 1 and 2 Corinthians, Philippians, Colossians, 1 and 2 Thessalonians, Philemon, the apostle associates others with himself in the address. These Epistles are seven in number (Feature 7), and their order numbers, 53, 54, 57, 58, 59, 60, 65, have for their sum 406, or 58 sevens (Feature 8).

In 1 and 2 Thessalonians, with order numbers 59 and 60, Paul associates with himself two persons, whereas in the others he has only one. Accordingly, the number 406, or 58 sevens, is thus divided: 1 and 2 Thessalonians have 119, or 17 sevens; the other Epistles have 287, or 41 sevens (Feature 9).

The three associates of Paul are Silvanus, Sosthenes, and Timothy. These names occur respectively in the New Testament 2, 16, 24 times: 42 in all, or 6 sevens (Feature 10).

Of the 66 order numbers of the books of the Bible, or 6 elevens, every eleventh number is: 11, 22, 33, 44, 55, 66; their sum is 231, or 7 x 11 x 3. This number is not only itself a multiple of seven as well as of eleven (Feature 11), but the sum of its factors, 21, is also a multiple of seven, it being 3 sevens (Feature 12).

21. The number of Old Testament writers named as such is 21, or 3 sevens (Feature 13), of which 14, or 2 sevens, are not named in the New Testament as Bible writers, and seven, as shown above in Sec. 5, are so named (Feature 14). These seven writers occur in the Old Testament 2,310 times, a multiple of both seven and eleven, it being 7 x 11 x 2 x 3 x 5 (Feature 15); while the sum of its factors, 28, is 4 sevens (Feature 16).

Of these 2,310 occurrences the writer whose name occurs most, David, has 1134, or 7 x 3 x 3 x 3 x 3 x 2, not only itself a multiple of seven (Feature 17), but the sum of its factors, 21, is 3 sevens (Feature 18). Again: Moses, the first Bible writer, has 847, or 7 x 11 x 11, a multiple of both seven and eleven (Feature 19). And this number is thus divided: the books which have this name less than ten times have 77, or 7 x 11; the others have it 770 times, or 7 x 11 x 10, also a multiple of both seven and eleven (Feature 20).

The Old Testament books which belong to

authors of more than one book are: Exodus Leviticus. Numbers. Deuteronomy. Proverbs. Song of Songs. Ecclesiastes,—seven in number (Feature 21). The sum of their order numbers. 105, is 15 sevens (Feature 22). And of this number Moses has 14, or 2 sevens; and Solomon has 91, or 13 sevens (Feature 23). And of Solomon's three books again Proverbs has 28, and the Song of Songs and Ecclesiastes have 63, or 9 sevens (Feature 24).

22. It was seen above in Sec. 18 that these seven Old Testament writers have for the sum of the books in which their names occur 99, or 9 elevens. That is to say: the numbers for the books of the seven Old Testament writers named in the New are specially marked off, so that their sum should be so many *elevens*. A similar design is marked off for the New Testament writers themselves, only the number here is *seven* instead of eleven. For the names of the New Testament writers occur thus: James is found in 11 books, Peter in 8, Jude in 8, Paul in 15, John in 7; in all 49, or 7 sevens (Feature 25). Their order numbers are 45, 46, 47, 51-65, their sum 1,008, or 144 sevens (Feature 26).

23. The chance for these 26 features of sevens being here undesigned, merely accidental, is about one in 81,472,966,297,612,001 x 16,807; the chance for these sevens to merely happen at the same time with those 24 features of elevens enumerated above is only one in a number of some *forty-five figures*. And the above enumera-

tion of the features of sevens and elevens is in nowise exhaustive.

One other feature, however, may be pointed out. The Old Testament consists of 39 books, or 3 *thirteens* (feature 27). Now this number is thus divided: the Law and the Prophets (see Sec. 5) have 26 books, or 2 thirteens; the "Writings" have thirteen (feature 28). And again: the anonymous books are thirteen, the non-anonymous are 26, or 2 thirteens (feature 29).

Of the 27 New Testament books, or 3 nines, nine are anonymous; and 18, or 2 nines, are non-anonymous; (feature 30). So that as in the whole Bible the proportion between anonymous and non-anonymous books is one third for the one and two thirds for the other, so the same proportion is kept up in the two Testaments separtely.

In connection then with the mere three items of the number of Bible books, their order numbers, and the names of some of its writers, highly elaborate schemes of seven and eleven are observed along with other minor numeric features, all of which are clearly designed.

24. Before proceeding to inquire just who the designer of these numerics is, some of the important consequences may be pointed out which necessarily follow the discovery of elaborate numeric design here.

The Bible of a large portion of Christendom, the Roman Catholic, consists of more than 6' books, the so called Apocrypha forming a part thereof. As the numeric design, however, is destroyed in every one of its fifty-odd features by the addition or removal of even a single book, the numeric design thus *acts as a check against any attempt to tamper with the designed* NUMBER *of the books.*

The Roman Catholic Bible is, therefore, wrong in admitting books that were clearly not designed to form part of the Bible.

As many of the numeric features run through the *order numbers* of the Bible books, their particular order as given in the Hebrew for the Old Testament, and in the Greek for the New, is clearly designed: since a number of the features are lost in the order of the English Bible. The numeric design is thus found to act as an *effectual check against any attempt to tamper with the designed* ORDER *of the* 66 *books.*

The Protestant Bible, therefore, though right as to the number of the 66 books, is thus wrong in their arrangement.

25. A striking illustration of the effectiveness of the numeric design in preserving the exact order of the books as originally designed is furnished by features 5, 11 and 21-24. Secs. 11, 14, 20, above. It will be noticed that the three books of Solomon are not kept together in the original, as in the English, but the order is: Proverbs, Job, Song of Songs, Ruth, Lamentations, Ecclesiastes. Now every consideration of mere *human* wisdom is against such a separation of these three books from each other.

But those features of the design are possible only with the present arrangement of the three Solomonic books. And the seeming restoration of order here in the English Bible is only doing violence to careful elaborate design. "The Scripture cannot be broken" even in the matter of the mere order of its books.

26. Coming now to the question, Who is it that put this design thus into the Bible, let just the single case of the name of Moses be considered:

The Old Testament was written by at least 21 different writers; the New, by at least five. So that the Bible, according to its own testimony, was written by at least 26 different writers. The whole of the Old Testament was translated from the Hebrew into Greek as early as some 280 years before Christ. As the New Testament could not have been written before the Crucifixion in A. D. 30, some 300 years thus lie between the writing of the two Testaments.

It could indeed be shown that between the writing of his books by Moses and the writing of Revelation by John not indeed three but some *sixteen* centuries must have passed; but for the present purpose the particular number of centuries does not matter. Enough if it be established that between the writing of the two Testaments there lie—centuries.

Let the reader now turn to Sec. 17, and look once more at the phenomena there presented by the name of Moses alone, to say nothing at present of the other names.

27. If the Bible writers themselves are the ones who planned this distribution of the name Moses with its double scheme of sevens and elevens, how did they contrive to accomplish it? Only by an understanding among the 26 different writers of the 66 different books so to insert this name in their writings that it shall be found in all of them just 7 x 11 x 11 times with several other features of sevens and elevens. This implies that Moses began this scheme deliberately, expecting that subsequent writers after him, some of them following him *only after centuries*, would insert his name just enough times to keep the design in suspense,—yet always in full view by each writer—until it gets to John, who by using it in his Revelation just once at last completes the centuries ago planned and waited-for design.

Merely to state it thus is to say at once that 26 men writing centuries apart, and living in different lands, could have had no such understanding among themselves. Such an understanding, if had, could originate, be kept up for centuries and finally carried out only by a miracle, and moreover by a continuous miracle.

28. One other possibility remains: Some one may have revised the whole Bible in such a manner as to distribute deliberately the name Moses among its different books so as to produce these numeric schemes. It must clearly be either some one who lived after Revelation, in which book Moses is found; or its writer,

John himself; since without this one occurrence of Moses in Revelation this elaborate numeric design is—destroyed. But the Hebrew text of the Old Testament was already settled centuries before John; the text was most zealously guarded by the Jews even to its jots and tittles; and since the numeric schemes run through both Testaments as a unit, the alterations in the text must have been made by a hated Christian. So far as to the impossibility of deliberately altering the Old Testament; yet the numeric scheme, if deliberately put into the Bible thus positively demands such alteration. Any tampering, however, with the text of the New Testament, even by the apostle John himself, would be rebuked at least by the Diotrepheses of his day who did not shrink even from refusing to receive him. Moreover, for the purpose of carrying out the numeric design alterations in the New Testament without any in the Old would be of no avail. And even apart from these considerations nothing short of miraculous skill would be required for carrying out this design even in the case of the name of Moses alone. David's case with his 1,134 occurrences presents, however, the same need of miraculous skill; the same is true of the rest of the seven names which form a special group with Moses and David, in Secs.5, 14, 16-17, 20-21. And again several of the numeric features run already *through the Old Testament alone independent of the New.*

29. On mere human grounds, therefore, these numeric phenomena, even those of the name of

Moses alone, are simply inexplicable. And this
is the case of only one in thousands. The
hypothesis that these numeric phenomena got into the Bible by the design of man thus proves
equally impossible with the hypothesis that they
are due to mere chance.

There thus remains the only explanation that
to rational minds presents no difficulty whatever: that a MATHEMATICAL MIND SUPERIOR TO
MAN, *the Great Mathematical Builder of Nature*,
has planned and executed His Volume of Revelation on exactly the same design as His Volume of Creation as planned. Only those who
deny that there is at all an Intelligent Creator of the world, and those who deny that such
a Creator *would* write a book thus, can turn
away from this the only explanation of these
otherwise wholly inexplicable facts. But to thus
turn away from facts, and from the most ele-
mentary laws of Logic is to stamp oneself not
as a rational but as an irrational mind.

II.

30. Having thus presented the case so that
readers of the mere English Bible can see and
verify the facts for themselves, a few additional
facts may now be presented which, while equally
important, can be *verified* only by those who
know Hebrew and Greek.

[In the following discussion the texts used
are: for the Old Testament, the Received Hebrew text; for the New, the Greek Revision by
Westcott & Hort.]

31. Neither the Jews nor the Greeks had any separate signs for numbers corresponding to our Arabic figures. The letters of their alphabets are used instead. Each Hebrew or Greek word is thus an arithmetical sum of the numeric values of its letters. Accordingly, the numeric values of the names of the writers to whom the Bible books ascribe themselves are:

345	Moses	21	Haggai
401	Isaiah	242	Zechariah
271	Jeremiah	101	Malachi
156	Ezekiel	14	David
381	Hosea	375	Solomon
47	Joel	95	Daniel
176	Amos	278	Ezra
91	Obadiah	113	Nehemiah
71	Jonah	833	James
75	Micah	755	Peter
104	Nahum	685	Jude
216	Habakkuk	781	Paul
235	Zephaniah	1069	John

The sum of these 26 numeric values of the Bible writers' names, 7,931, is 11 x 7 x 103: not only a multiple of eleven (Feature 31), as well as of seven (Feature 32), but the sum of its factors, 121, is also a multiple of eleven, it being 11 x 11 (Feature 33); and of these writers Paul, who has the largest number of books, has a numeric value of 781, or 71 elevens (Feature 34).

Of the 7 Old Testament writers named as such in the New (Sec. 5) Moses is the first and Daniel the last. Their numeric values are 345 and 95, together 440, or 11 × 2 × 2 × 2 × 5,—a multiple itself of eleven (Feature 35), and the sum of its factors 22, or 2 elevens (Feature 36).

32. If now against the 44 non-anonymous books, or 4 elevens, be placed the numeric values of their authors, we have the following:

2	345	Exodus	33	375	Ecclesiastes
3	345	Leviticus	35	95	Daniel
4	345	Numbers	36	278	Ezra
5	345	Deuteronomy	37	113	Nehemiah
12	401	Isaiah	45	833	James
13	271	Jeremiah	46	755	1 Peter
14	156	Ezekiel	47	755	2 Peter
15	381	Hosea	51	685	Jude
16	47	Joel	52	781	Romans
17	176	Amos	53	781	1 Corinthians
18	91	Obadiah	54	781	2 Corinthians
19	71	Jonah	55	781	Galatians
20	75	Micah	56	781	Ephesians
21	104	Nahum	57	781	Philippians
22	216	Habakkuk	58	781	Colossians
23	235	Zephaniah	59	781	1 Thessalonians
24	21	Haggai	60	781	2 Thessalonians
25	242	Zechariah	62	781	1 Timothy
26	101	Malachi	63	781	2 Timothy
27	14	Psalms	64	781	Titus
28	375	Proverbs	65	781	Philemon
30	375	Canticles	66	1069	Revelation

The sum of these 44 values, 18,843, is 1,713 elevens (Feature 37); of which the writers of more than one books, Moses, Solomon, Peter, and Paul, have 14,168, or 1,288 elevens; and the

22 writers of only one book, or 2 elevens, have 4,675, or 425 elevens (feature 38). And once more: the numeric value of the writers of the books that stand at the head of the 7 divisions of the Bible, Moses, Isaiah, David, James, John, is 2,662, or 11 x 11 x 11 x 2, a multiple of eleven (feature 39) elevens (feature 40) of elevens (feature 41).

33. The Bible begins with the word *B'reshith*, "In Beginning." It ends, in Westcott & Hort's revision, with the Greek *hagion, of saints*. The one is a form of the noun *Reshith*, 'beginning'; the other, of the adjective *hagios, holy,* hence *saint*. Now the Hebrew word *beginning* occurs in the Old Testament 51 times; the word *hagios, saint,* occurs in the New 235 times; the two together occur thus in the whole Bible 286 times, or 26 elevens (feature 42). The Hebrew word has six letters, and the Greek has five. The two words then with which the Bible begins and ends have eleven letters (feature 43). The Hebrew word in this particular form occurs five times; the Greek word occurs 39 times; the two words together thus occur in the Bible 44 times, or 4 elevens (feature 44). The Hebrew word occurs in Genesis, Isaiah; the Greek word occurs in Matthew, Mark, Luke, Acts, 2 Peter, Romans, 1 and 2 Corinthians, Ephesians, Colossians, 1 Thessalonians, Hebrews, 1 Timothy, Philemon, Revelation. The order numbers of these books are: 1, 13, 40, 41, 42, 44, 47, 52, 53, 54, 56, 58, 59, 61, 62, 65, 66; and their sum is 814, or 74 elevens (feature 45). The reputed writers of

the *anonymous* books in this list are Moses for Genesis; Matthew, Mark, and Luke, for the first three Gospels; and Paul for the Epistle to the Hebrews. The numeric values of the names of these five writers are 345, 340, 431, 721, 781; and their sum is 2,618, or 238 elevens (Feature 46), or 7 x 11 x 17 x 2, a multiple moreover of seven as well as of eleven. Of these five writers Paul is the only one who is a writer of both anonymous and non-anonymous books in the above list; the numeric value of his name, 781, is 71 elevens (Feature 47).

If we now place against each of the above 17 Bible books the numeric values of their writers, reputed and acknowledged, the numbers are: 345, 271, 340, 431, 721, 721, 755, 781, 781, 781, 781, 781, 781, 781, 781, 781, 1069; their sum is 11,682, or 1062 elevens (Feature 48). And this number is thus divided: the two Old Testament writers have 616, or 56 elevens; the New Testament writers have 11,066, or 1,006 elevens (Feature 49), 616 being moreover a multiple of seven as well as eleven.

34. The numeric value of the one Hebrew word *In the Beginning*, with which the Bible begins, is 913, or 83 elevens (Feature 50). While the word with which the Bible closes, *hagios, holy* or *saint*, of which *hagion, of saints*, is a plural form, is found in the books having these order numbers: 40, 41, 42, 43, 44, 46, 47, 48, 51, 52, 53, 54, 56, 57, 58, 59, 60, 61, 62, 63, 64, 65, 66. The sum of these numbers is 1232,

or 112 elevens (Feature 51). This number is made up of four groups each of which consists of only consecutive numbers: thus: 40-44; 46-48; 51-54; 56-66. Now the number 1232 is thus divided: groups 1-3 have 561; or 51 elevens group 4 has 671, or 61 elevens (Feature 52). And again: the order numbers of the anonymous books in this list are 40, 41, 42, 43, 44, 48, 61. So that the number 1232 is thus divided: the anonymous books have 319, or 29 elevens; the non-anonymous books have 913, or 83 elevens (Feature 53).

35. The sum of the numeric values of the 26 Bible authors named therein as such was seen above in Sec. 31, to be 7,931, or 7 x 11 x 103, a multiple of *seven* as well as eleven (Feature 54). Of this number 1,414, or 202 sevens, belong to Moses, the first writer of the Bible named therein as such, and John, the last named therein as such; and 6,517, or 7 x 7 x 7 x 19, belong to the other writers, a multiple of seven (Feature 55) sevens (Feature 56) of sevens (Feature 57).

This number 7,931, is moreover thus divided by sevens: the 21 writers of the Old Testament, have 3,808, or 544 sevens; and the New Testament writers have 4,123, or 589 sevens (Feature 58).

Of the number 3,808, the sum of the values of the Old Testament writers, or 544 sevens, 2,933, or 419 sevens, belong to the Law and the Prophets, from Moses to Malachi; and 1,190, or 170 sevens, belong to the Hagiagrapha so

called, from David to Nehemiah (Feature 59).
And of this last number 1,190, or 170 sevens,
14, or 2 sevens, belong to David, who heads
this division; and 1,176, or 7 x 7 x 24, a multiple
not only of seven but of its square, belong to
the other writers of that division (Feature 60).

With reference to the fact that seven of the
Old Testament writers are named as such in the
New, this number 7,931 is thus divided by
sevens: these seven writers have for their
numeric value 1,554, or 222 sevens; the other
writers have for theirs 6,377, or 911 sevens
(Feature 61).

Of the value 4,123, or 589 sevens, belonging
to the writers of the New Testament, James,
the first in order, has 833, or 7 x 7 x 7 x 17, a
multiple not only of seven but of seven sevens,
and 3,290, or 47 sevens belong to the other
writers (Feature 62).

The sum of the order numbers of the books
in which the last word of the Bible occurs,
1,232 (See. 34), is also a multiple of seven as well
as of eleven, it being 7 x 11 x 16 (Feature 63).

36.   The Hebrew word with which the Bible
begins occurs in the books having the following
order numbers: 1, 2, 3, 4, 5, 8, 12, 13, 14, 15,
17, 20, 27, 28, 29, 33, 35, 37, 39, nineteen
books. The books in which is found the word
with which the Bible ends, with their order
numbers, are given above (See. 34), twenty-
three books.   These two words thus occur in
42 books, or 6 sevens (Feature 64); and the sum

of their order numbers is 1.575, or 225 sevens (Feature 65). In Sec. 34 it was already shown that the anonymous New Testament books of these 42 books have for the sum of their order numbers a multiple of eleven. Now the sum of the order numbers of the Old Testament books here is 77, or *eleven sevens* (Feature 66).

37. The word with which the Old Testament begins has just been seen to occur in 19 books; the word with which the Old Testament ends, in the Hebrew, *alah*, "to go up," with a numeric value of 105, or 15 sevens (Feature 67), occurs in 11 books, being found in every book except Ezra and Esther. The two words then with which the Old Testament begins and ends are found the one in 19 books, the other in 37; their sum is 56, or 8 sevens (Feature 68); and the sum of the order numbers of the books in which they occur is 2,051, or 293 sevens (Feature 69).

The numeric values of the Hebrew forms with which the Old Testament begins and ends, *B'reshith* and *V'yaal*, are 913 and 116; their sum, 1,029, is 7 x 7 x 7 x 3; a multiple of seven (Feature 70) sevens (Feature 71) of seven (Feature 72).

The word with which the Bible begins, *Reshith*, occurs therein in 10 different forms 51 times. Now the numeric value of all the occurrences of this word is 46,942, or 6,706 sevens (Feature 73); while of its 10 forms those without a prefix have a value of 2,793, or 7 x 7 x 19 x 3.

a multiple not only of seven, but of seven sevens (Feature 74). And the form *Reshith*, distinguished both as occurring the largest number of times and without either prefix or suffix, occurs 28 times, or 4 sevens (Feature 75).

38. These additional numeric features of sevens and elevens by no means exhaust the enumeration of the numeric phenomena obtained so far from so to speak merely scratching the surface. One further specimen, however, of the manifold numeric wealth that lies scattered here, there, and everywhere on the surface of Scripture, may now be given as a last example: It was stated in Sec. 35 that the numeric value of the five New Testament writers named therein as such is 4,123, or 7 x 19 x 31, a multiple of seven in combination with *nineteen* and *thirty-one* (Feature 76). Now the value of the words *biblos hagion, book of saints*, with which the New Testament begins and ends, is 1,178, or 19 x 31 x 2—the same combination of 19 x 31 (Feature 77). The chance for this feature alone even being accidental is only one in 693,253.

And while speaking of the combination of seven with *nineteen*, let the reader look back to the preceding page: the value of the forms of *Reshith* which have no prefix is there seen to be 2,793, a multiple of nineteen as well as of seven (Feature 78). And that this is part of the general numeric scheme is shown by the fact that the number of letters in all the occurrences of these forms without a prefix is 152, or 8 nineteens (Feature 79).

39.   In Sec. 24 we have already seen that the numeric design thus forever settles the *number* and *order* of the books of Scripture.   The 79 additional numeric features discussed in Secs. 32-38 not only confirm what Secs. 10-29 teach, but they give us additional and final information on several hitherto much disputed matters:

(*a*) The numeric values of the writers named as such in the Scriptures show that their number was *designed* to be just 26, neither more nor less. *This at once settles the question of two Isaiahs.* The phenomena of Bible Numerics are wholly incompatible with the notion that there are two writers for the one book of Isaiah.

(*b*) The elaborate theories of some modern "scholars" about the Jehovistic, Elohistic, Deuteronomic, and Priestly documents which are supposed to make up the works of Moses, are also wholly incompatible with the facts of Numerics which clearly show that Moses was *designed* as the writer of at least four of the books ascribed to him.

(*c*) But Bible Numerics settle the authorship not only of the books whose writers are named as such in Scripture, but also of the *anonymous* books.   Features 48-66, on pp. 48-51, show conclusively that it was part of the *design* that Genesis have Moses for its author, Hebrews have Paul, and the first three Gospels have Matthew, Mark, and Luke for their writers, and Acts have Luke for its writer.

(*d*) The Revised Version gives *Amen* as the last word of Scripture, without even intimating

that some authorities omit the word. Westcott
& Hort, on the other hand, omit it, without
any notice whatever of *Amen* as a possible alter-
native. So that with them Scripture ends with
hagion, of saints. Tischendorff, Alford, and other
critical editors differ about *saints*: some having
with the Authorized Version *all* instead of *saints*.
Now of these three different readings that of
Westcott & Hort alone falls in with the numeric
design, as shown by features 50-53 and 64: so
that no fewer than *twelve* numeric features
would be lost by the change of a single word.
So true once more is the saying of the Lord
The Scripture cannot be broken.

40. It was shown in the preceding pages
that an elaborate scheme of *sevens* and *elevens*
runs through the whole Bible in connection
with the number and order of its books, and the
occurrences, numeric values, and distribution
of the names of its writers. Incidentally it has
already been seen that at least in some of the
numeric features the two Testaments have each
sub-designs of their own. Thus while the first
and last words of the whole Bible, for example,
display striking numerics (Secs. 34, 36), the
words with which each Testament separately
begins and ends show the same phenomena (Secs.
37-38). The same is true of the division between
anonymous and non-anonymous books (see Sec.
23).

Let us now look a little more closely at the
New Testament separately:

III.

41. The New Testament books, with their own order numbers, are:

1	Matthew	15	2 Corinthians
2	Mark	16	Galatians
3	Luke	17	Ephesians
4	John	18	Philippians
5	Acts	19	Colossians
6	James	20	1 Thessalonians
7	1 Peter	21	2 Thessalonians
8	2 Peter	22	Hebrews
9	1 John	23	1 Timothy
10	2 John	24	2 Timothy
11	3 John	25	Titus
12	Jude	26	Philemon
13	Romans	27	Revelation
14	1 Corinthians	378.	

42. The sum of the 27 order numbers is 378, or 54 sevens (Feature 80); of which the first and the last have 28, or 4 sevens (Feature 81). The New Testament itself, as already stated, names only 5 writers for 18 of its books, the other 9 being anonymous. But there is good evidence that Matthew and Mark wrote the first two Gospels; that Luke wrote the third and Acts; that John wrote the fourth and three of the Catholic Epistles; and that Paul wrote Hebrews. Order numbers 1, 2, 6, 12, thus belong to writers of only one book, the others belong to writers of more than one. The sum of the 27 order numbers, 378, or 54 sevens, is then thus divided: 357, or 51 sevens, belong to

writers of more than one book: and 21, or 3 sevens, belong to writers of only one book (Feature 82): and this number is moreover thus divided among the four numbers of which it is the sum: the first and the third have seven: the second and fourth have 14, or 2 sevens (Feature 83). Again: among the Epistles and non-Epistles the number 378 is thus divided: the six non-Epistles have 42, or 6 sevens: the 21 Epistles have 336, or 48 sevens (Feature 84). And of this last number the Catholic Epistles have 63, or 9 sevens: those of Paul have 273, or 39 sevens (Feature 85). And again: the numbers of the seven Epistles in which Paul associates others with him in the Title are: 14, 15, 18, 19, 20, 21, 26. Their sum is 133, or 19 sevens (Feature 86): and of this sum the first numebr has 14, or 2 sevens (Feature 87).

In conection with this last number, 133, or 7 x 19, let the reader turn back to Features 76, 78-79. See. 38. As there so here also there is a little scheme of nineteens beside the sevens, thus: the middle number of the seven which make up the sum 133, or 19 x 7, is nineteen (Feature 88); while the two numbers on each side of it have for their sum 38, or 2 nineteens (Feature 89).

Of the Epistles some are addressed to individuals: namely: 2 John is addressed to Kyria (Lady): 3 John, to Gaius: 1 and 2 Timothy, to Timothy: Titus, to Titus: Philemon, to Philemon. The order numbers of these Epistles are: 10, 11, 23, 24, 25, 26. Their sum

is 119, or 17 sevens (feature 90): of which John
has 21, or 3 sevens; and Paul has 98, or 14
sevens (feature 91).

Most of the Epistles are addressed either to
some named person, or to some unnamed persons dwelling, however, in some named place.
To this latter class belongs also 2 Peter. For
though in the superscription neither person nor
place is named, the writer says in that Epistle,
"This *second* Epistle write I unto you." But
the first Epistle is addressed to those in "Pontus, Galatia," etc.; so that the second Epistle
is thus also addressed to them. Now the Epistles that have neither person nor place in the
address are James, 1 John, Jude, Hebrews, with
order numbers 6, 9, 12, 22. Their sum is 49,
or seven (feature 92) sevens (feature 93): of
which the first and last have 28, or 4 sevens;
and the two middle ones have 21, or 3 sevens
(feature 94).

43. Of the New Testament writers named
theirein as such, James, Peter, Jude, Paul, John,
Peter and Paul expressly name themselves as
Apostles. The sum of the 27 order numbers,
378, or 54 sevens, is accordingly thus divided:
the 15 books that assign themselves to these
two apostles have 266, or 7 x 19 x 2, a multiple
not only of seven (feature 95) in combination
with nineteen, but the sum of its factors, 28, is
4 sevens (feature 96); and the other books
have 112, or 16 sevens.

Of these other books the order numbers 1,

4, 9, 10, 11, 22, 27, belong to writers who are apostles according to the good evidence furnished outside of the New Testament itself: that is, the apostle Matthew is credited with the first Gospel: the apostle John with the fourth, three Epistles, and Revelation: the apostle Paul with Hebrews. The books thus credited to apostles, though on authority extraneous to the New Testament, are seven (Feature 97): the sum of their order numbers is 84, or 7 x 2 x 2 x 3, a multiple itself of seven (Feature 98), and the sum of its factors is 14, or 2 sevens (Feature 99). And of this number Gospels—Catholic Epistles have 35, or 5 sevens: and Hebrews-Revelation have 49, or seven (Feature 100) sevens (Feature 101).

There are thus as many as 22 distinct features of sevens in the mere item of the order numbers of the New Testament books as distinct from the order numbers of these same books when treated as part of the whole Bible.

44. In Sec. 35 it has already been noted that the numeric value of the five New Testament writers named as such therein is 4,123, or 7 x 19 x 31: of which number the first writer, James, has 833, or 7 x 7 x 17. Here are these five names in the Greek: *Iakob* (of which *Iakobos* is only a form), *Petros, Ioudas, Paulos, Ioanes*. The sum of their numeric values, 4,123, or 589 sevens, is thus divided: 210, or 30 sevens, belong to the first and last letters of the list: 3,913, or 508 sevens, belong to the remaining letters (Feature 102).

45.   It was seen above that in the matter of numeric values the five New Testament writers are divided as it were into two classes: James forming one, the other four writers forming the other.   Now of these four names, the first and last letters in each have for their sum a multiple of seven: thus *Petros, Peter,* 80 and 200, or 280, which is 40 sevens: *Ioudas, Jude,* 10 and 200, or 210, which is 30 sevens.   In *Paulos, Paul,* and *Ioanes, John,* it is again 280 and 210 (Feature 103).   Only the following letters are used in these four names: *a, d, e, ē, i, l, n, o, p, r, s, t, u, ō,* with numeric values of 1, 4, 5, 8, 10, 30, 50, 70, 80, 100, 200, 300, 400, 800. The number of these letters is 14, or 2 sevens (Feature 104); of which seven are vowels, and seven are consonants (Feature 105); their numeric value is 2,058, or $7 \times 7 \times 7 \times 6$, a multiple not only of seven, but even of its cube (Feature 106).

46.   As to the first of these five names James, it presents these phenomena: Just seven persons have this name *Iakob, Iacob* or *James:* (1) the patriarch; (2) another ancestor of the Lord in the genealogy of Matthew; (3) the apostle, son of Zebedee; (4) the apostle, son of Alpheus; (5) brother of the Lord, writer of the Epistle; (6) the brother of Joses, called the Little; (7) the father of the apostle Judas not Iscariot, or Thaddeus (Feature 107).   Of these seven persons the five that belong to the New Testament period occur therein 42 times, or 6

sevens (Feature 108); of which the son of Zebedee, has 21, or 3 sevens; and the other four have the other 21 (Feature 109). While the writer James is mentioned in Matthew once; in Mark once, in Acts thrice, in James once, in Jude once, in 1 Corinthians once, in Galatians thrice. The order numbers of these books are: 1, 2, 5, 6, 12, 14, 16. These books are seven in number (Feature 110), their order numbers have for their sum 56, or 8 sevens (Feature 111), of which the books having the name more than once have 21, or 3 sevens, and those having it only once have 35, or 5 sevens (Feature 112). And of those 35 Paul has 14, or 2 sevens, and the other writers have 21, or 3 sevens (Feature 113). And the sum of these seven order numbers, 56, is moreover thus divided: the numbers under ten have 14, or 2 sevens; those over ten have 42, or 6 sevens (Feature 114). And if against each of the 11 occurences of this James the order number of the book be placed, the sum is found to be 98, or 7 x 7 x 2 (Feature 115).

47. Every seventh book of the New Testament is written thus: the 7th, 1 Peter, by Peter; the 14th, 1 Corinthians, and the 21st, 2 Thessalonians, by Paul. The numeric values of their writers, if placed against these books, are: 755, 781, 781, with their sum 2,317, or 331 sevens (Feature 116). And as the New Testament consists of 27 books, or 3 *nines*, the same scheme is carried through every *ninth* book thus: 1 John, Philippians, Revelation, are every ninth book.

The numeric values of their own names,
John, Paul, John, are 1,069, 781, 1,069, . . .
sum is 2,919, or 417 sevens. For . . . 417 . . .

48. Some of the Epistles themselves . . . the
the manner in which they are written: whether
by amanuensis or by the writer himself. Thus
1 Peter is written through S. anus . . . rough
Silvanus, the faithful brother, as I . . . him.
I have written unto you briefly." Romans is
written through Tertius; "I, Terti . . . wr . e
the Epistle, sal . e you." by 1 Corinthians,
Colossians, and 2 . . . ssalonians, it says, "The
salutation . . . me . . . me with . . . me own hand,"
thus telling us t . . . es . . . are letters were dic-
tated, the salutation alone being autographic.
On the other hand Galatians and Philemon expressly describe themselves as written by the
apostle directly; "See with how . . . letters I
have written unto you with mine own hand,"
in Galatians "I P. . . d write it with mine own
hand, I will repay . . ." in Philemon.

Now the Epistles that thus themselves des-
ignate t . . . m . . t their writing are seven in
number . . . '48. While the two *autograph*
letters, Gala . . . . nd Philemon, have for their
ord r ma . . . . and 26, together 42, or 6
s . . . s . . . 49. The numeric values of
. . . v . . . nses, *Silvanus* and *Tertius*,
or . . . *ane* . . . *rtius*, are 1,031 and 985, to-
. . . . 946. . . . 288 sevens feature 120 .

. . . ne acknowledged and reputed New
. . . at writers are Matthew, Mark, Luke,

John, James, Peter, Jude, Paul: *Maththaios,
Markos, Loukas, Ioanes, Iakob, Petros, Ioudas,
Paulos.* These 8 names have 49 letters, or
seven (Feature 121) sevens (Feature 122); of
which the first and last have 14, or 2 sevens; and
the others 35, or 5 sevens (Feature 123). The
names of the four non-apostles Mark, Luke,
James, Jude, occur in the New Testament respectively 8, 3, 69, 46, times, in all 126, or 18 sevens
(Feature 124); of which the first and third have
77, or 11 sevens, and the second and fourth
have seven (Feature 125) sevens (Feature 126);
and the names occurring the largest and smallest
number of times, Paul 158, and Luke 3, occur
together 161 times, or 23 sevens (Feature 127);
while the numeric values of the writers of only
one book, Matthew, 340, Mark, 431, James, 833,
Jude, 685, have for their sum 2,289, or 7 x 3 x
109, itself a multiple of seven (Feature 128),
and the sum of its factors, 119, is 17 sevens (Feature 129).

There are thus a large number of distinct
features of sevens in connection with the mere
item of the numeric values of the names of the
New Testament writers.

50. But in addition to these features of
sevens, since the number of New Testament books
is 27, or 3 nines, there are also features of nines
here. It has already been pointed out (Sec. 23,
Feature 51) that the division between anonymous and non-anonymous books is by nines. The
acknowledged and reputed New Testament

writers are eight: Matthew, Mark, Luke, John, James, Peter, Jude, Paul. Of these the first four writers have nine books, and the other four have 18, or 2 nines (Feature 130).

The sum of the 27 order numbers, 378, is a multiple of nine as well as of seven, it being 9 x 7 x 6. And this number is thus divided by nines: the first four writers, Matthew, Mark, Luke, John, have the order numbers 1, 2, 3, 4, 5, 9, 10, 11, 27, with the sum of 72, or 8 nines. The other four writers have 306, or 34 nines (Feature 131).

51. Some of the New Testament books are designated in their name by a *number*: 1 and 2 Peter; 1, 2, and 3 John; 1 and 2 Corinthians; 1 and 2 Thessalonians; 1 and 2 Timothy. Their order numbers 7, 8, 9, 10, 11, 14, 15, 20, 21, 23, 24, have for their sum 162, or 9 x 9 x 2, a multiple not only of nine, but even of its square (Feature 132); and of this sum Peter and John have 45, or 5 nines, and Paul has 117, or 13 nines (Feature 133). The numeric values of the three *persons* thus named here, if set against their books, 755, 755, 1,069, 1,069, 1,069, 704, 704, are seven (Feature 134), and their sum is 6,124, or 7 x 7 x 5 x 5 x 5, a multiple not only of the square of seven, but also in combination with a cube, presenting a geometrical figure (Feature 135).

52. Of the first four New Testament writers Matthew, *Maththaios*, has written one book, of which the order number is 1; and his name has

8 letters. Mark, *Markos*, has also written one, with the order number 2, and has 6 letters. Luke, *Loukas*, has written two books, with the order numbers 3 and 5, and has also 6 letters. John, *Ioanes*, has written five books, with their order numbers 4, 9, 10, 11, 27, and has also 6 letters. If now the number of letters in the name of its author be placed against each of these nine books, their sum is found to be 56, or 8 sevens (Feature 136); of which Matthew and Mark have 14, or 2 sevens, and Luke and John have 42, or 6 sevens (Feature 137). And if the number of letters of each author be placed against each book and multiplied by its order number, the sum of the nine numbers is found to be 434, or 62 sevens (Feature 138); of which Matthew and Luke have 56, or 8 sevens; and Mark and John have 378, or 7 x 9 x 6, a multiple of both seven and nine (Feature 139).

A look at the New Testament independently of the Old reveals thus no less than 60 numeric features, mostly of sevens, which number, however, is by no means exhaustive.

53. It was already seen in Sec. 39 that several supposedly unsettled questions about the Bible are effectually settled by Bible Numerics. They reduce to that much waste paper the elaborate and lengthy discussions about the authorship of the Pentateuch, of Isaiah, of Hebrews. And moreover, though the Bible itself does not directly give us the authorship of the first three Gospels and Acts, its numerics fully confirm

Tradition in naming Matthew, Mark, and Luke as the writers of these four anonymous books (Sec. 33).

In Sec. 24 it was likewise seen how the status of the Apocrypha is effectually settled as an alien and sheer intruder into the Bible. The true order of the books, and the true ending of the Bible were also found to be definitely established by Numerics. All this from features 1-79 above. Let us now see what additional information is to be got from the other features.

54. The first thing to be noted is that the 60 new features obtained independently of the others confirm in every detail all the conclusions already arrived at with regard to the New Testament. The true order of its books is confirmed by nearly all of the new features; the true authorship of Matthew, Mark, Luke, Acts, and Hebrews, is also confirmed by many of the new features. But in addition to this independent confirmation of the results already obtained, these 54 new features settle a number of hitherto supposed doubtful matters:

55. Though two-thirds of the New Testament books, eighteen of them, ascribe themselves to definite authors, their authorship has been in one way or another extensively denied or doubted; in some cases even by those of the household of faith. Most of Paul's Epistles have thus been doubted. It has been doubted or denied that the author of John, 1 John, 2 John, 3 John and Revelation is the same, even

if the name of the different writers be John. It has been doubted whether Peter wrote more than one Epistle; whether the writers of Luke, James, and Jude, lived in the apostolic age. In fact, not a book but what has in its turn thus been doubted or denied.

Of all this Bible Numerics makes short work, as is readily seen by a few examples:

(a) The fourth Gospel, though its writer is not named, is by an *apostle* (See. 43, features 95-101; see also See. 49); and by one who wrote more than one book (See. 42). Now the only four apostles who are New Testament writers are: Matthew, Peter, Paul, John. The fourth Gospel must have been written by one of these four. But not by Matthew, since he was the writer of only one book, as shown by features 82, See. 42, and elsewhere. Neither was it written by Paul, since according to its own account in the last chapter this Gospel was written by one of the twelve. Nor by Peter, since in both the last chapter and the account of the Last Supper Peter is distinguished from the "disciple whom Jesus loved," to whom the Gospel assigns itself. John is thus established by Numerics as the writer of the fourth Gospel, even though in the New Testament itself it is anonymous.

(b) In like manner it was shown in See. 50 that Matthew, Mark, Luke, and John wrote between them nine books. It is established in See. 49 and elsewhere that Matthew and Mark wrote each only one book; seven therefore belong to

Luke and John. But some features show that only an apostle could have written the five books ascribed to John. And as Luke was not an apostle. Numerics thus establish the apostle John as the only possible writer of these five books: and they again reduce to that much waste paper the numerous lengthy and contradictory discussions about their authorship.

(e) Features 133-135. Sec. 51. establish among other things that Peter wrote two Epistles. And a little attention to these and the other features shows that every disputed matter of New Testament authorship is finally settled thus:

That Matthew the apostle wrote the first Gospel: Mark, the second: Luke, the third and Acts: John the apostle, the fourth, three Epistles and Revelation: James, brother of the Lord, his Epistle: Peter, the apostle, his two Epistles: Jude, his Epistle: Paul the apostle, 14 Epistles.

56. This and much like information is obtained so far by merely scratching the surface of the Bible. Only the number and order of the books, and the names of their authors, have so far been examined. The text itself has been barely touched. But not only are these numeric phenomena presented by the Bible as a whole, and by each of the two Testaments separately, but it can be readily shown that similar schemes are found not only in any book of the Bible, but also in any one item of any one book. Let that one book be Judges, for example, and let that one item be the number of years mentioned therein.

Well, there are just 22 such numbers of years in Judges, or 2 elevens; having for their sum the number we have already met in the case of Moses (See. 16), 847, or 7 x 11 x 11, the combination of seven with the square of eleven; with over a dozen other features of sevens and elevens to be observed in those 22 numbers.

Matthew 1: 18-25, the story of the birth of our Lord; Mark 1: 1-8, the account of John Baptist; Acts 6: 1-7, the story of the first deacons, have each a vocabulary of 77 words, or 7 x 11, with elaborate schemes of sevens and elevens in each case. It will presently be seen how the single word *luo, to loose,* the discussion of which is taken up for another purpose, displays an elaborate scheme of sevens and elevens. Other examples might be multiplied.

With regard to this frequency of the sevens in combination with the elevens it is to be observed that calling the difficulty of constructing a scheme of sevens *sevenfold,* it becomes in combination with eleven *seventy-and sevenfold.*

57. With these facts before us the contention of modern critics that the Bible having been written by men is a *merely* human production, and is to be treated "like any other book," is unsound. Holy Writ is *unlike* any other book, is *not* the work of mere man, and is *not* to be treated "like any other book." Rather is it, Put off thy shoes from off thy feet, for the place whereon thou standest is holy ground. And again, Living is the word of God,

and active, and sharper than any two-edged sword. . . . .

One or two examples will now be given of the value of Bible Numerics in its application to matters *outside* the Bible.

IV.

58. In taking a list of the 29 forms in which the word *luo, to loose*, occurs in the New Testament, the writer used Geden's Concordance. The number of letters in these forms is there 185, or 37 × 5; the number of letters in all the occurrences of the 29 forms is there 262, or 131 × 2. Neither of these numbers shows Bible Numerics. The forms being 29 in number, it occurred to the writer that the total number of letters is probably one less, 261, or 29 × 9. The final *n* in the dative plural of nouns and in the third person of verbs always needs examining. The forms *luen, lusen*, were accordingly examined for the perhaps superfluous *lusen* occurs before a word beginning with a vowel, so its *n* was beyond suspicion. But when the writer came to *luen* in John 5: 15, he found that Westcott & Hort actually omit the *n*, and that Geden failed to record that fact, because he takes no notice of differences between Tischendorff and Westcott & Hort in mere matters of spelling. *But its retention breaks up an elaborate numeric scheme.*

59. The numerics of this word are these: Its forms are twenty-nine (.eature 1), which

have in all their occurrences **261** letters, or **9** twenty-nines (Feature 2). Of these the forms in *du* have **29** (Feature 3); those in *luo*, **29** (Feature 4); and the remaining forms have **203**, or **29 x 7**, a multiple of both twenty-nine and seven.

The word occurs **42** times, or **6** sevens (Feature 5), of which the largest occurrence is in Luke, seven times (Feature 6). The Gospels and Catholic Epistles have **28**, or **4** sevens; the other divisions have **14**, or **2** sevens (Feature 7). Its forms have the following numbers of letters: **4, 5, 6, 7, 8, 9, 10**. Their number is **7** (Feature 8); their sum is **49**, or seven (Feature 9) sevens (Feature 10); of which the middle number has **7** (Feature 11); the first and last have **14**, or **2** sevens (Feature 12); and the numbers on each side of the middle one have respectively for each pair together also **14** (Feature 14). The numeric value of the two letters of which the prefixes to the forms are made up *l, o* is **35**, or **5** sevens (Feature 14). The value of the longest form, *luthesontai*, is **1078**, or **7 x 7 x 11 x 2**, a multiple not only of seven, but of its square in combination with eleven (Feature 15).

A scheme of sevens as well as of twenty-nines thus runs through this word.

60. The first letter of this word has the **11th** place in the alphabet, the second has the **20th**, the third has the **24th**. The sum of these places is **55**, or **5** elevens (Feature 16), of which the

first has 11, and the other two have 44, or 4 elevens (Feature 17). The total numeric value of all the 42 occurrences of this word is 34,518, or 11 x 2 x 3 x 523, itself a multiple of eleven (Feature 18), and the sum of its factors, 539, is 11 x 7 x 7, a multiple of both eleven and the square of seven (Feature 19). Of this number the first form due has 440, or 40 elevens (Feature 20), and the last has 1,430, or 130 elevens (Feature 21). The word occurs in Matthew 6 times, in Mark 5, Luke 7, John 6, Acts 6, 2 Pter 3, 1 John 1, 1 Corinthians 1, Ephesians 1, Revelation 6. The numbers thus used for the occurrences 1, 3, 5, 6, 7, have for their sum 22, or 2 elevens (Feature 22); while if against each occurrence be placed the number of letters in the name of the writer of its book, the number of letters is 264, or 24 elevens (Feature 23).

61. This does not exhaust the numerics of this word. In addition to these schemes of sevens, elevens, and twenty-nines, there are also schemes of sixes and seventeens. But enough has been given to show that an error in a Concordance is detected almost at a glance by means of Numerics. They spoke as it were. Seek for the intruder, and the intruder is found, now to be rejected forever.

When from a knowledge of the laws of the heavens Adams and Leverrier were enabled to say just where in the heavens a missing planet was to be looked for, the finding thereof shortly after did no more for the truth of the science of Astronomy than this finding of the superfluous *n* in the Concordance does for Numerics.

62. Incidentally the phenomena of *luo* settle two hitherto doubtful readings: In 1 John 4:3 even Westcott & Hort are uncertain whether *annulleth Jesus* should not replace *confesseth not Jesus: luei* for *me homologei*. But Numerics are against the change. In Revelation 1:5 Numerics justify the Revisers' change of *loosed, lusanti* for *lousanti, washed.*

V.

63. The diameter of the moon is given as 2,163 miles, or 309 sevens. The mean diameter of the earth is given as 7,917 miles, or 7 × 13 × 29 × 3. The diameter of Venus is given as 7,630 miles, or 1,090 sevens; and that of Mars as 4,998 miles, or 7 × 7 × 17 × 6. Of the nine bodies that move round the sun (the eight planets and one of their moons) nearly half have thus diameters the numbers of whose miles are multiples of seven. The diameters of Neptune and Uranus are not known as accurately; but those of Mercury, Jupiter, and Saturn, are given as 3,009, 89,769, and 73,044 miles. Each of these numbers comes within just *one* of being a multiple of seven; 89,768 being even a multiple of seven sevens. It is reasonable therefore to assume that there is an error of just one mile for each of these planets. But if so, this error, observe, is detected and corrected *solely by Bible Numerics.* And the Bible, instead of being proved

false by Astronomy proves itself to be the final arbiter in these data of Astronomy.

64. Mercury turns around on its axis in 24 hours, 5 minutes, 30 seconds, or 86,730 seconds. This is 7 x 7 x 1770, a multiple of seven sevens. Jupiter turns thus, according to Airy, in 9 hours, 55 minutes, and 21 seconds, or in 35,721 seconds. This is 7 x 7 x 9 x 9 x 9, again a multiple of seven sevens, and in combination with the cube of a square. The moon of Neptune turns on its axis in 5 days, 21 hours, 3 minutes, or 8,463 minutes. This is 7 x 13 x 31 x 3. The sidereal year of the earth is 365 days, 6 hours, 9 minutes, 9 seconds, or 31,558,149 seconds, or 7 x 9 x 5,000,923. The sidereal periods of the four moons of Uranus, if added together, give 2,491,272 seconds, or 7 x 8 x 9 x 4,943, of which the first three moons have 1,328,040, or 7 x 8 x 9 x 17 x 31 x 5; and the fourth has 1,163,232, or 7 x 8 x 9 x 4 x 577. Each of these three numbers is a multiple not only of seven, but also of 8 x 9.

Now the earth turns on its axis in 23 hours, 56 minutes, and 4 seconds, or 86,164 seconds: again only one over 7 x 11 x 3 x 373, a multiple of both seven and eleven. Mars turns on its axis according to Proctor in 24 hours, 37 minutes, and 22 seconds, or 88,642 seconds, also within only one of 7 x 7 x 3 x 3 x 3 x 67, a multiple of the square of seven combined with a cube. And once more, the four moons of Jupiter have for the periods of their sidereal revolutions together 2,519,742 seconds. This number again is within only one of 359,963 sevens: of which, as in the case of Uranus, the fourth moon has 1,441,860, or 205,980 sevens; and the other three have 1,077,881, or 153,983 sevens. It is reasonable, therefore, to suppose, the approach in all these cases to a multiple of seven being always within *one* second, that the true numbers are here also multiples of seven; and that there is some uniform cause for this aberration of one second either in the instruments, observers, or methods of computation.

Science may thus yet find itself obliged to have recourse to the Bible, hitherto rejected as "unscientific," for the final verification of its own numeric data.

A word in conclusion. *Verbal* Inspiration of the Scriptures is now so effectually abandoned, even among the professedly orthodox, that not a single "scholar" nowadays holds it. And even to profess to try to prove it is sufficient cause in the estimate of "scholars" for refusing even a hearing for it. It must be remembered, however, that the *logical* conclusion of no-verbal inspiration is anti-Christian rationalism. The Lord Jesus, the Apostles, the early Church, and the true Church of all ages, have firmly held that all and "every Scripture is inspired of God." That some even devout scholars could see their way to strenuously oppose verbal Inspiration only shows that their logical power was inferior to their piety and learning. And in these days above all it must be remembered that a sin against Logic, specially in a leader of men, may become in the sight of God as heinous as breaches of the decalogue. Vicious logic has more than once made an outright murderer of an otherwise well meaning soul. And it cannot be affirmed too solemnly that if not *wholly* inspired to its every letter, the Book is not an anchor of Christian hope, but a spider's thread. From an unshakable assurance it becomes a plaything for the guesses of the latest "scholar." If error *is* possible in even a single word of the Bible that word may as well be in the Lord's saying "Who believeth and is baptized shall be saved," as in the Inscription on the Cross, for example. So that, for aught we know, the Lord's true saying may be, "Who disbelieveth shall be saved: who believeth and is baptized shall be—condemned." On its own principles modern "scholarship" (much of it only Guessership) cannot say that this is impossible. Of course the supposition is silly, but modern scholarship has propounded, fought for, believes itself and has led the multitude to believe many a thing about the Bible more unreasonable than this.

But after all the real question here for the reader is not what ever shifting scholarship "thinks," but what he is going to *do* about it. The fact of Numerics is there. Scholars may ignore it, but the Sun still shines, whether scholars ignore it because in their beds during the short night, or in their graves during the long one. The ostrich hiding his head in the sand was never deemed type of intellectual candor. And on the Great Day every one shall give his *own* account for heedlessly passing by the burning bush lighted expressly by a God calling unto him. I want thine attention. The plea that "scholars" told me that burning bushes are "of no importance" will not avail *then*, the law of Heaven being. If blind lead blind *both* fall into the ditch. Not the mere blind "scholar," but also the in his own estimation doubtless innocent follower.

NOTE.

From time to time the writer receives printed articles in which their writers amuse themselves with imagining that they overthrow Numerics: by irrelevant comparisons, deceptive facts, defective logicisings, and if need be just by ridicule or a smart sneer. Correspondents send such things to the writer always in the hope, often in the expectation that he will "answer" all such. The writer's time is very limited, and it is a well known maxim that one momentary foolish objection may take days to refute, if refuted it ever is at all.

The writer lets all such things alone. Those who have *honest* difficulties with Numerics can always apply to him personally for explanation. His writings are not hidden away, nor does he himself play hide and seek with seekers after information. The writer's address is always given in all his writings. The very fact that objectors rush into print there to display their lack of apprehension of the subject at once stamps them as unworthy of the writer's attention, whether the objector be a "Reverend Professor" contributing regularly to a London weekly, or a mere illiterate pamphleteer who thinks it needful to print his own (badly taken) photograph as one of his "arguments" with which to refute Numerics.

Truth is never served, certainly not Christian's truth by "arguing" with anyone, least of all with those who show that they know not whereof they speak.

Numerics are a test not only of the Christian Scriptures, but also of Christian character. One who L-o-v-e-s God's book *rejoices* in Numerics even though he understands next to nothing thereof. He joys even in the glimmer it affords of the majesty of God's Book, of the wondrousness of the work of the Spirit. One, however, who merely *likes* the Book, but *likes* other things just a little more (*his* ideas, *his* notions, theories, schools, *his* wisdom, attainments, and the rest) will take to Numerics just in proportion to his lack of completion of the Master's image in him. He may accept it as true, but will wait for "Have the rulers also believed on him?" before *he* commits himself to Numerics publicly. He may ignore it altogether as "unworthy" of *his* (darling) conceptions of what the Bible in his estimation *ought* to be, the question of what it really is being of course of secondary importance before MY idea of the Bible: the big *my* being the fatal flaw in the character of such a one

If there is some secret worm gnawing away at his spiritual vitals, then such a one will calmly sit down, and send to the press "refutations" of Numerics. . . . . .

But all such do not need "answers" at all. What they do need is that the good Lord in His mercy humble them, and show them their poverty and blindness; and they can be benefitted more by being prayed for in secret than by being discussed in public.

It can be safely accepted as a fact whenever a Christian is indifferent or lukewarm, and specially when he is opposed to Numerics, it is always due to a sort of intellectual incompetence behind which lurks some spiritual weakness, often an emasculation if not a down-right atrophy along certain lines of Christian life. This is indeed pitiful, but the sad truth is that on God's great day Numerics will rise as a swift witness against many a one who does not even suspect that he had slightingly passed by a Burning Bush lighted for him by a merciful God to attract his attention. . . . . . .

WS - #0113 - 230623 - C0 - 229/152/5 - PB - 9781528321495 - Gloss Lamination